Riding on the Coattails of Genius

Riding on the Coattails of Genius

Two Decades Aboard Dell's Pioneer Ship

JOHN C. CAMPBELL

Riding on the Coattails of Genius Copyright © 2018 by John C Campbell. All Rights Reserved.

Contents

	Dedication	vii
	Acronyms - Easy Reference Guide	ix

Part I. Signing on with Dell Direct

1.	Boarding the Dell Ship	2
2.	Streamlined and Built for Speed	5
3.	Next Stop, "The Internet"	9
4.	Riding the Waves	14
5.	How the Internet Revolution Rocked my Boat	23
6.	A Small Detour	28

Part II. The Partner Side of the Ship

7.	Thawing the Giant Iceberg	34
8.	Building a Bigger, Better Ship	39
9.	Charting New Waters	46
10.	Diving with an "A" Team at LVAR Island	51

11.	A Quick Tour of the Partner Side of the Ship	58
12.	Wrapping up the Trip	65

Part III. In Summary

13.	Michael	70
14.	Where I Did Not Go	78
15.	Disembarking the Dell Ship	81
	Afterword	88
	Author Note	93

Dedication

This is a story about my own journey aboard the fast-moving, ever-evolving Dell juggernaut, where I was always surrounded by the most extraordinary people:

To my fellow Technical Sales Reps: You all are my family. Even today, whenever I meet a new TSR we still tend to see eye to eye.

To the hundreds of Sales and Field Reps I supported as a TSR: I loved the teamwork and appreciated you all!

To my managers, the good, the bad, and the exceptional: I learned something important from each of you. From Jason to Mae and everyone in-between, Thank You!

To the thousands of Account Execs, Sales Engineers, Directors, VPs, and Owners at the hundreds of Partners I supported for more than a decade at Dell: I really enjoyed showing you the value of Dell and helping you take care of your customers.

Finally, to all the contributors who helped make this book happen. May you all live long and prosper!

And in particular...

A special "Thank You!" to Maria, my manager for almost a decade in the Partner Division and friend for life. You supported me when I was sick, kicked me in the pants when I needed it, and always showed me the right way to do things.

Bernie, you are my friend and mentor.

Tracy, you are the best of the best. Every day we worked together was a productive pleasure.

Alvin and Fadi, you are geniuses in our industry and friends for life, "One for All and All for One!"

Jim, it would have been a much shorter, less interesting ride without your creative caring.

Sam, believe it or not, I paid attention to everything you said and learned something important every time.

Michael Dell, you made the whole journey possible. We all ride on the coattails of your genius.

— John

Acronyms - Easy Reference Guide

Divisions:

SMB = Small and Medium Business
DCS = Dell Custom Solutions
DSC = Dell Solutions Center
EBC = Executive Business Center
LVAR = Large Value Add Reseller
PG = Product Group

Roles:

SE = Sales Engineer
AE = Account Executive
TSR = Technical Sales Rep
IPS = Inside Product Specialist
ISR = Inside Sales Rep

Server and Storage:

JBOD = Just a Bunch of Drives
SAN = Storage Area Network
DAS = Direct Attach Storage

Miscellaneous:

DOMS = Dell Order Management System
OME = Open Manage Essentials
OEM = Original Equipment Manufacturer
FRS = Field Readiness Seminar
IOT = Internet of Things
AI = Artificial Intelligence
LOB = Line Of Business
SOP = Standard Operating Procedure
POV = Point of View
FUD = Fear, Uncertainty, and Doubt
ASAP = As Soon As Possible
DARPA = Defense Advanced Research Projects Agency

PART I
SIGNING ON WITH DELL DIRECT

For most of the years I worked at Dell, I was a single father raising my only son and needed a role that didn't demand travel.

I had already "been there and done that," so working all day handling issues, motivating low achievers, and navigating the politics of the place as a manager was not as attractive to me as depending on the fruits of my own efforts.

I opted for an inside role at something I've always been good at, Sales. It was simply more fun and more lucrative for me to spend my days taking care of customers' needs.

The bonus was, I got to go home most nights satisfied.

Of course, as a single father, the burnout that so often plagues those in sales was not an option for me.

Somehow, I managed to survive for more than two decades in the trenches, on the front line that is sales.

1. Boarding the Dell Ship

In January of 1995, after some years at the helm of my own small ship, Campbell's Computer Connection, my very pregnant wife demanded I find a job that produced a steadier paycheck. The money made building and selling my own brand of computers meant there was no financially-pressing need to act, but her wish was my command. Since Dell was the most sought-after employer in the Austin area (then, as now) I decided it was "Dell or Bust" for me.

A beautiful blonde baby boy was born into our world in March of that year. We named him Kent to honor one of our favorite people in the world, my own cool cousin, Kent, who was living a laid-back life at the time in his own houseboat at a dock on Lake Travis.

It took until December to finally land a job with Dell's consumer-oriented Catalog Sales Division. I walked through the doors of Dell's headquarters in Round Rock, Texas at the start of their next quarter on February 5th, 1996.

My younger more carefree years had been spent jumping from one sales job to the next. Whether it was sales to businesses, homes, retail, wholesale, on the phone, or face-to-face, I was interested in every form of sales. I even tried my hand at selling a "Zig" Ziglar-like program designed to train a company's employees to become better salespeople. After several dozen sales jobs in the 70s and 80s, I had spent the last decade running my own companies.

I was confident I could make money anywhere, so how did I end up staying twenty-two years at Dell, only leaving to help one of Dell's largest Partners figure out how to sell more Dell?

Maybe, because I was never bored at Dell. Or, it could just be that I became a true, blue-bleeding Dell believer along the way. What I really think justified my continued passage on that mighty ship was the fact that I stayed in sales generating ever-bigger revenues and making better paychecks during that entire exciting trip into always-new directions.

And what a journey it was!

In those early days, Dell housed their entire sales force in one large building called Round Rock One. It was just east of Interstate 35 in Round Rock, a small city north of Austin. There was a Walmart, McDonald's, and a Mexican food restaurant just to the west of us next to the Interstate, but the view out my window was mostly open country.

It wasn't long before cranes were hoisting the two- and three-story walls of Round Rock Two into place. Today, there are six large sprawling buildings on the massive campus that is the Dell mothership. That campus is surrounded in turn by multitudes of shopping centers, restaurants, and the many neighborhoods composed in large part of present and former Dell employees.

And that's just at the mothership itself. I can't begin to guess how many hundreds of properties Dell owns worldwide. As of mid-2018, estimates are they have to support a total of 138,000 Dell Technologies employees, as well as all the operations required to generate what should be close to eighty billion dollars in sales before the end of their next fiscal year.

2. Streamlined and Built for Speed

Dell was already a powerhouse company when I joined. Through the turn of the century and on into this millennium, Dell ran roughshod over its competition. Michael's company made good solid products, and without the drag of a traditional supply chain, Dell's Direct model meant our computers were about half the price of those our larger competitors such as HP and IBM were selling.

Early on, I took a tour of Dell's new factory which was just down the road from our headquarters. I remember standing on an interior balcony with a panoramic view of the entire facility spread out before me, marveling at its efficiencies.

Trucks were backed up to a dozen large bays on my left, disgorging their contents straight onto long assembly lines that pretty much covered the floor. I knew the parking lot beyond was full of semis from different vendors. The ones I was seeing had just won the bidding war for that day, earning them the right to pull up to our doors and unload their products, be it processors, memory sticks, hard drives, or other common components.

The average length of time we held any part in inventory before it moved onto the production line? About four hours. Michael called it his "just in time" inventory system.

As soon as each system was built, it was loaded into one of the racks of testing bays that ran along the entire right side of the factory floor. Just beyond where all those newly constructed computers were being burned in, another dozen large doors were open revealing truck beds being loaded with well-engineered, high quality, fully tested systems that had just been boxed for shipment to our customers all over the country.

How good were our prices and products back then? I remember one customer who called and told me, "I'll buy fifty laptops if you can get me a ten percent discount."

I had to respond, "Neither I, nor my manager, are allowed to discount our systems." The truth was we didn't need to provide additional discounts to sell our products. If quality was important to a customer, there were simply no better deals than the ones they received in the mail from what the media was calling, "That little catalog computer company in Texas."

As Dell salespeople, we were all pulling in big bucks back then. There were a hundred of us on the floor taking orders as fast as we could, with typically fifty to a hundred customers in the queue waiting to talk to us from the beginning to the very end of our day.

Our parking lot was full of luxury vehicles, and I remember more than one employee bemoaning the ultimate cost of a new kitchen floor or patio deck because Dell stock had split so many times since they sold their shares to finance that home improvement. In fact, so many employees got rich in the 1990s the media took to calling them "Dellionaires."

Bill Gates himself showed up at one of our annual meetings in the Austin Convention Center. One of his slides showed how well Microsoft stock had done over the years. Then he threw up another slide showing Dell stock's meteoric rise in value next to Microsoft's steady but comparably slow uphill climb, and he told us Dell was the one stock they couldn't compete with. The truth was, he admitted, they couldn't even come close. That brought him a thunderous roar of applause from the mere five thousand of us that made up Dell in those halcyon days.

HP, IBM, Compaq, Packard Bell, even copycat companies like Gateway and Micron couldn't match the efficiencies of the Dell model or the quality of our desktops and laptops. Gateway and Micron faded from the computer manufacturer scene over the years. HP and Compaq stumbled into each other's arms. Even mighty IBM eventually ended up selling off its x86 business and retreating to its mainframe roots.

3. Next Stop, "The Internet"

About a year into supporting the catalog sales calls coming in on Dell's consumer-oriented queue, I was asked if I wanted to join a team being put together to support the Internet.

Now, that may sound like an obvious choice in retrospect, but stepping away from that never-ending queue with its line of customers stacked up just waiting to buy, to join a team taking calls from a new, relatively untested queue was not such an easy decision at the time.

I went ahead and made the jump, but I have to admit I had a little insider information. Paul was a good friend of mine. He was also the single sales rep supporting all Internet sales at Dell up to that point. Paul had talked me into going into sales instead of support when I first applied at Dell, so I had a tendency to listen to him when he told me to jump on this new opportunity ASAP.

That first team turned into two, then into a dozen.

Management started calling us the "Super Queue," and we were growing so fast they never could quite pin down our quotas. Almost immediately, we generated a million dollars in a single month, and Dell's Internet revenues grew exponentially the entire two years I was there.

We were supporting the earliest versions of what everyone today calls "The Internet," and I got to talk to some of the most interesting people.

I remember one scientist working at a famous lab who called in to buy three or four high-end Precision workstations. We got to talking about the Internet, and he mentioned he was actually one of its creators. He told me it was a DARPA project initially, and I could hear his wink over the phone when he admitted all the people on his team were really hippies at heart, and that when they designed their new invention they knew there was no way it could ever really be controlled by the military.

Another person who ran one of the IT departments for a major university told me they had already purchased more than fifty Dell computers, and not one of them had broken, ever.

Mom and pop were not coming to us through that

Super Queue back in the first few years of Internet sales at Dell. It was all scientists, heads of IT, CEOs of companies, and similar smart and tech-savvy characters. They might be calling to purchase a single laptop or a dozen.

For me, it was a fun and extremely profitable adventure at the cutting edge of tech, and it taught me I could "break the bell curve" at Dell by trying new things, a lesson I took to heart. In fact, that particular experience motivated many of my future directions at Dell. I am going to discuss what "breaking the bell curve" really meant to me in the next chapter, but first I want to revisit an old friend. Its name was DOMs.

DOMs, the Dell Order Management System, was our order entry database. It ran on Tandem servers, and the code for it had been written way back when there were only about sixty employees at Dell. The screen we used to build out a customer's system had a box for every component, and we entered codes that matched to the choices each customer made, what speed processor, how much memory, what size hard drive, and so on.

Although it was cryptic and very grueling for all new reps to learn, it was as fast as shorthand once you got the hang of it. To finish a sale we took a customer's payment info, then hit a key combination that actually placed the order. That order transferred directly to our manufacturing floor for almost immediate build out.

DOMs was so dependable we used it for twenty of the twenty-two years I was at Dell. On the rare occasions when it went down, I simply pulled out a yellow legal pad, made notes on everything, and told the customer I'd call them back with their order confirmation in a few hours. No matter what, we had to keep taking orders. I used to joke with my customers saying, "I can remember one time when we slowed down. It was on Christmas Eve from 2:00 to 3:30 in the afternoon. Then we got busy again."

I was in sales for a long time before joining Dell. Spending half my day cold calling was just part of the downside of being a salesperson. Each hard-bought lead was like gold to me. At Dell, it never stopped raining gold. We had trouble getting back to anyone who told us, "I just want to think about it," because that next potential buyer was already waiting in the queue.

After I moved to the Super Queue, I remember one strategy: after following up with a customer a couple of times with no response, I would make one more call and leave a message saying, "This is John Campbell with Dell. Sorry I missed you again. I don't want to keep bothering you, so I won't call anymore. If you are still interested in the system we built, please don't hesitate to give me a call. I am always happy to help."

Most of the time they called back pretty darn quick to let me know that they were still very interested in the system, and could I please continue to hold on to their quote. More often than not, I answered a couple of questions that were bothering them and ended up closing the sale while we were still on the phone. Giving away a potential customer with a tactic like that would've been unthinkable in my pre-Dell days. Even with calls coming in almost on top of each other, it may have been a bit of a gutsy thing to do, but it was a lack of time, not any lack of care that created that particular strategy.

4. Riding the Waves

Dell was more like a port town than any sort of civilized place back in the 1990s, and our sales floor was full of adventurers. Everyone did everything they could to rack up revenues, trying to "break the bell curve."

Our quota was a monthly number reflecting the average attainment of our entire floor the month before. On a bell chart, that would be the hump in the curve. The trick was to work smarter and/or harder than Dell was counting on, because everything over our expected attainment earned four times the payout. In other words, if I reached a hundred and twenty-five percent of my quota for the month, I exactly doubled the size of my paycheck. If there were still shipping days left in the month, reaching that hundred percent mark also meant it was time to double-down on overtime.

There was an actual graphic of a thermometer on our pay screens showing a red line that "heated up" along with our daily sales revenues. If we went way over a hundred percent, that red would actually burst out the top of the thermometer in a geyser that guaranteed our next paycheck would be anywhere from significant to massive.

Our own conscience dictated how we dealt with our customers to earn those bigger paychecks. I remember one young hotshot in the Catalog Sales Division. When a caller didn't buy immediately, he would say, "If you give me your credit card info, I can put what we just built on hold until you are ready to make a decision." After they hung up, he would go ahead and place the order. He never answered his incoming calls either. They would roll over and his teammates would end up getting an earful as they tried to soothe, then move a very irate caller over to customer service to set up the return.

The trick to his tactic was, since Dell was rock-solid and only about half the price of our competition, only about half his customers actually returned their new desktop or laptop when it, quite unexpectedly, arrived on their doorstep.

That young man had figured out a valid way to break the bell curve and make a larger paycheck. It may have been a short-sighted strategy on his part, but he did make a bunch of money for a little while, then he was gone.

Very few chose that kind of mercenary tactic. One, because most people are inherently decent. Two, because Dell was a dream job. In those days it was far more carrot than stick, and I am pretty confident all our type A personalities came to work every morning thinking about how to break that bell curve. I know I did.

As I write this, I am looking at the October 1997 issue of *Sales and Marketing Management* magazine. A very professional and relaxed-looking Michael Dell is on the cover. In that issue, they rated the sales forces of all the top companies, and you can guess who was Number One.

At the time the article came out, I was the highest grossing salesperson on the biggest revenue generating Super Queue team at Dell. I told my mom that made me the Number One Salesperson in America. She bought it, but hey, she's my mom.

The truth is, I was still a new dad, and that responsibility weighed on me. I averaged seventy-five hours a week on the job, brought a sack lunch to work every day, and when I had to break long enough to go to the restroom, I ran. Sales has always been a game of numbers. Talk to more customers and you make more sales. That's all there is to it.

Not every year was that good, and there were umpteen changes in the way we got paid with way too much drama around each. I just worried about the number on my W-2 at the end of each year, but even my occasional off year was colored by my curiosity. There was so much going on at Dell, so much potential being realized, that I always wanted to stick around to see what would happen next.

Perhaps more importantly, the vast majority of the people I worked with were fun to be around. So many kids did, and still do, graduate from the University of Texas and want to stay in Austin, that Dell has a huge talent pool to draw from. In addition to our UT grads, there were ex-pro athletes, former business owners and leaders, and along the way, a large influx of folk from other countries.

Dell became a highly diverse environment over time, but most everyone shared one common trait: they were almost all invariably sharp individuals. Before I came to Dell, I was used to seeing most of my coworkers put in their hours just to get to the weekend. But, the main force of Dell's employees was always highly motivated, and we all typically worked well together with a common goal: taking care of Dell's customers. It was exciting to be around, and it kept me on my toes.

It's worth taking a moment here to stop and revisit the quota system itself. In sales for two decades before joining Dell, my previous jobs had all been commission based. Since I was used to getting paid a percentage of revenues and was typically near the top of the sales ranks, I loved commission sales. To me, it always looked like blue skies and no limits all the way to the horizon. When I joined Dell, I didn't really understand what a beautiful tool quotas were for limiting a salesperson's income.

Consider this: whenever I grew my sales, my quota adjusted upward commensurately. If I generated 30K a month for Dell one year and the next year averaged 300K, my quota grew right along with my revenues. It meant I should always be struggling to meet quota, and if I only met quota, my income would stay relatively flat over the years. If Dell was raking in ten times more profit due to my efforts, that was simply good for the company.

It wasn't a Dell thing, just something I hadn't dealt with up to that point in my life. I ended up living under Dell's quota system for fifty-plus quarters and came to understand, since employees are a company's biggest cost, that quotas are the best invention ever for any company. I know they have been the standard recompense engine for sales reps in large corporations ever since that first evil genius came up with the idea, oh so many bottom lines ago, but (and it's an all-important "but") there is always a way to beat the system and break the bell curve.

In the first few years I was at Dell, it was as simple as I described earlier. If the majority of sales reps averaged 300K a month, find a way to sell 400K, 500K, or more. It didn't stay that easy though. Dell has always been a stat factory. As the company grew, quota calculations became far more complex.

For example, one quota would be calculated for one rep supporting a particular set of customers and a different quota for the next. Then, the pencil pushers at Dell got really smart. They started applying an inherently hypothetical "growth" number on top of each quota.

No matter how Dell finessed the statistics, there was always a way to sell more than the historical measures said you could. On that ship of great and ongoing opportunities, there was always that next new way to blow out the thermometer and take home a massive paycheck.

It wasn't all about finding new opportunities within Dell, either. When working with any particular account set, a little out-of-the-box thinking could produce wonderful results.

For example, when I was in the Super Queue, I was having a hard time asking all the probing questions Dell wanted me to cover at the start of every call. It was upsetting to the person calling in, since they couldn't ask for what they wanted until they gave me what I needed, and it was frustrating for me as well.

Then, I found that if I just asked a couple of basic questions that showed my interest in their world, the person on the other end of my line would respond positively, a conversation would ensue, and with no friction, I would end up getting all my required questions answered.

Since there was no pressure and I wasn't taking up too much of their time, my customers were happy to talk about their work and their challenges. It got to where it only took a few minutes to fit my probing requirements into any conversation, and I was building a much better rapport along the way than I ever had reading from a script.

Our main measure at that time was revenue generated against number of queue calls. Callbacks placed directly to an extension were not included in that measure. When they were ready to buy, my customers had a tendency to call me back instead of just calling into the queue (also to refer their friends to me and, if a reseller, to become a friend and regularly call to order), so I ended up making more sales than my queue calls allowed.

With a close rate that exceeded one hundred percent, as Dell measured it, I had successfully outperformed that particular metric. Since I was also skewing the numbers for the entire floor, when I was ready to move to my next role, the Super Queue managers breathed a sigh of relief and sent me off with their blessings.

Working smarter, not harder was another way to generate a bigger paycheck, but I do have to admit, at first there were some issues with the left turns my more maverick thinking took.

For example, I used to steer my customers away from leasing. I didn't really understand its value, so I didn't think of it as a good option for them. I can clearly remember a voice behind me one day ominously intoning, "Campbell, I hear you don't like leasing." When I turned around, the very tall, well-bulked, and athletic form of David, the head of our division, was looming over my desk with a frown on his face. That was actually scary.

In my second year at Dell, I had one of my most useful insights: unless my thoughts moved in the same general direction the company already wanted to go, my creativity would be pretty much wasted in a corporate environment. Although it might not seem like it on the surface, that was a very freeing revelation. Rather than making quick judgments or pulling strategies out of thin air, aligning my objectives to Dell's corporate goals gave me a solid underpinning for both my caring and my creativity, unleashing my power to become a more effective individual contributor.

The fact that Dell was constantly evolving gave me plenty of opportunities to ride the forefront of change and build new paths to success. My next role would take me, once again, in a new and very different direction.

5. How the Internet Revolution Rocked my Boat

In 1998, Michael Dell gathered all five thousand of us at Palmer Auditorium in downtown Austin to announce Dell was taking on the server market. He showed off our first three products: the PowerEdge 2100 and 4100 dual processor servers and the monster 6100 quad processor server. Michael told us the server market was living off bloated margins and highly proprietary designs, and that Dell was going to do something about both those costly facts.

Not long after that event, I interviewed for a new role that had been designed to help support those server lines. I was accepted and moved from the Super Queue over to SMB, the Small and Medium Business Division, to become a Technical Sales Representative or TSR.

TSRs are trusted advisors for just Dell's enterprise products, so I no longer owned the entire customer relationship. That was the job of the ISR, or Inside

Sales Representative. I supported an entire team of them. It didn't take long to get comfortable in my new role, because my ISRs proved to be really awesome teammates.

ISRs are, to this day, primarily responsible for the customer relationship. I say this, because in spite of all the good field people who come face to face with and do so many wonderful things for Dell's customers, these "chained to their desk" reps are the ones who handle all the minutiae of customer relationships.

They quote Dell client products, as well as coordinate all quotes from every specialty group. They apply for any discounts needed to help close a larger deal, then ride herd on orders and ensure any issues are ultimately resolved. They are masters of the detail, the good mechanics whose day is filled with turning the bolts, tuning the engine, and otherwise keeping our big ship running smoothly and on course for Dell customers.

When the TSR role was first introduced, there were only two of them supporting our entire division, Jim and Bernie. By the time I became a TSR, the Internet Revolution was picking up steam, and our division had eleven TSRs altogether. Jim had been promoted to our manager.

Even though I had successfully run Campbell's Computer Connection for half a decade before joining Dell, and already thought of myself as a technical person, when I went to my first TSR meeting, most of what was being covered went straight over my head.

In my first month on the job, in typical Dell fashion, I was tasked with helping design a twenty-five million dollar, three-tier Enterprise solution for an Internet startup. We had three weeks to deliver a design superior to our competition. There were so many components that had to mesh, my head would start spinning a few minutes into every conversation. Our new team muddled through and won the deal, mainly because we were supported by one of the high-level technical resources that are always available within Dell.

Despite the challenges, I relished the role from the first. When I became a TSR, designing technology solutions presented me with the same type of logic puzzles I had grown to know and love.

Some years earlier, during a short stint as a professional writer, I was typing away every day on my personal computer. When it stopped working, although I didn't know a thing about PCs, I was broke enough to try fixing it myself. Figuring out what was wrong ended up being one of the coolest puzzles I'd ever come across. When a friend's computer started acting up, I was just confident enough to try to help, and fixing that problem led to helping the next person.

Writing wasn't making me much money in the meantime. Kinda like a shade-tree mechanic, I eventually ended up teaching myself how to build and repair computers. Campbell's Computer Connection grew naturally out of those experiences. You could say, in a day when it was still unfashionable to consider oneself as such, that my true "geek" had been unleashed. My fascination with everything tech continues to this day.

The Internet Revolution steamrolled on. Month after month, our little team of TSRs averaged close to a hundred and fifty percent of quota.

Jim seemed to relish the challenges that came along with the nurturing of his little powerhouse team. He was a character who could look the impossible in the eye and dismiss it as only slightly improbable. Most of what I learned from him was by osmosis, as I watched him so capably handle his everyday challenges, and over the years, realized I was often emulating him. In everything he did, from how he handled our corporate realities, to the way he made things happen, even to how he taught a training class, I was a believer in Jim, just like so many others at our company have been.

Being as smart as a whip, Jim got very rich working at Dell. Last I heard, he was off hiking around the U.S., still a relatively young man but already retired.

The TSR title changed to IPS (Inside Product Specialist) a few years before I left, but everyone still calls them TSRs. Over the seventeen years I spent at Dell in that role, I supported literally hundreds of ISRs. Many of them have gone on to become product support specialists, managers, then directors, or have gone out into the field to take care of customers face to face.

6. A Small Detour

A few years into being a TSR, I was asked to run a special project for Microsoft. A product of theirs called "Small Business Server," or SBS, had a new release coming out, and they were ready to pay Dell to get a dedicated specialist assigned to that product. They wanted someone who could help improve SBS's relatively modest and long static attach rate of around two percent.

I went to Microsoft headquarters in Redmond for a week of in-depth training. The highlight of that trip was meeting and being instructed by the team responsible for developing that new version of SBS, called Small Business Server 2000. I returned with a clear understanding that SBS2000 was a quantum leap forward over its predecessors.

In previous generations of SBS, a loose bundle of Microsoft's most popular apps, including Exchange and SQL, were packaged with a server operating system. With the introduction of SBS2000, those same apps were streamlined to work better together and were more tightly integrated with Microsoft's new Windows Server 2000 operating system. Security for the network was thrown in for good measure. Friendlier and much less problematic all around, it was one winner of a product in my mind. I came back from Redmond fired up and ready to go.

My first big decision was an easy one. I figured I'd do a lot better getting help from my fellow TSRs than trying to accomplish anything game-changing on my own. I used my small advertising budget to buy other Microsoft products at a big discount and offered them as prizes to TSRs who were willing to focus on attaching SBS2000 to their server sales.

I also made myself an always-available expert in residence, so that when questions came up our TSRs could count on good answers. I was "Johnny on the Spot," ready to jump on customer calls with any TSR as needed. If I didn't have an answer to a question, I simply reached out to the SBS development team. Someone was always available and ready to help.

I came up with a flowchart that guided TSRs through their due diligence questions with simple yes/no choices to help determine if SBS would benefit the customer. Then, I got together with Scott, one of my fellow TSRs who also did videos for a wedding photography business he ran on the side. We came up with a series of training videos that featured me explaining how to use the flowchart and telling them which version of the Microsoft server OS would be appropriate for a particular customer.

The format was essentially the same as a newsletter I had already been writing for years called, "Servers Are Easy." It gained global distribution and won awards at Dell because (in the middle of their busy day) by the time a rep figured out if they needed to read it, they had already read it. In other words, simple, straightforward, and most of all, short!

That was about five years before the advent of YouTube. I liked the results so much I emailed Michael Dell a link to the videos. He actually responded within a few minutes, saying that he really liked the idea of "a two-minute, bite-sized training video."

He copied me on the follow-up email he shot off to his VPs around the world, sharing my video link, and challenging them to think of other content that could fit the same training format.

Sales started trending upward, but my real breakthrough came when I figured out the shine was coming off my Microsoft giveaways. Spiffs at Dell were so complicated at that time, that we often didn't know how we were doing until the dollars finally showed up in our paychecks (often after the spiff was over). I never found that very motivating, so never paid much attention to them.

For my next round of giveaways, I decided I was going to find a way to bring our TSRs some immediate satisfaction. I leveraged the glamour of Hollywood by driving to a Blockbuster video store and buying up several hundred used DVDs of some of the most popular movies of the time.

Every time a TSR sold a copy of SBS2000, I gave them a movie. What it really came down to was, they sold a twelve hundred dollar software bundle and I gave them an eight dollar movie, but that meant going by some TSR's desks and regularly dropping off a half dozen movies at a time.

Any TSRs who weren't selling Small Business Server saw this, and by the next week I'd be dropping movies off to them as well.

Mark, the Director at Microsoft who was responsible for my project, told me he would be happy with a six percent increase in SBS's long static attach rate. My stretch goal was nine percent. I actually increased SBS sales over two hundred percent!

Steve Ballmer, then CEO of Microsoft, sent me

kudos and decided to implement the same program in other parts of the world.

For a while, other TSRs were calling me from places like France and England. I could just picture my videos being played for those TSRs, showing them how to sell SBS2000 Texas-style.

That project taught me how to successfully promote a line of products for a large corporation. It also taught me how to track and report the results properly for executive consumption. Microsoft paid for a year of my time. Once the project was over, I went back to being a simple TSR and that was just fine by me.

PART II
THE PARTNER SIDE OF THE SHIP

We may have started out small, but over the dozen years I was TSR there, the growth of Dell's Partner Division was unrelenting.

Paychecks were above average, and the work was some of the most challenging and satisfying anyone could find at Dell.

7. Thawing the Giant Iceberg

If continuing to break the bell curve meant staying in front of the next wave of change at Dell, I never made a better decision than when I jumped ship from the Small and Medium Business Direct division to help open our new "Solution Provider" Partner division.

Dell had been Direct sales to customers for twenty years, when a small team of us went out to the National Reseller Convention in San Diego, in early 2003. Myself, our Director of Marketing, and a couple of other sales and marketing folk confidently introduced our new Value Add Reseller division to all the attendees. Our job was to tell them, "We don't want to steal business from you anymore, we want to do business with you!"

I do have to add that, when Mark, our Director, went up on stage to make the initial pitch, he paid a couple big bouncers twenty bucks each to go up there with him. Mark's icebreaker line, as he casually cocked a thumb over each shoulder at the bouncers, was, "We're here to do business with you, but just in case, these are my bodyguards." It received the laugh it richly deserved.

For years, Dell had been "The Devil" to resellers, as our Direct model regularly took the bread off their tables. Our prices were so hard to beat for so long, that going up against Dell with HP or IBM was often a losing proposition for them. Those Value Add Resellers, or VARs, came to us in droves when we opened our new Partner division; but in those first years we faced a daily battle to fight the deep-seated distrusts that had been brewing for two decades.

The new division consisted of myself as TSR and about fifteen of the smartest ISRs on our floor. We supported every Partner in the United States.

I only sold a handful of servers the first month we were in business, but that was fine by me. I was sure I had found a great new way to break the bell curve at Dell. After all, when they pitched this new division, it was by telling me that OEMs like Dell, IBM, and HP owned half the three-trillion-dollar technology market, but resellers owned the other half.

We quickly grew to 35 ISRs, with myself as the lone TSR. It was a double fistful of business for one TSR to handle. I knew the only way I was going see my little boy before he was put to bed each night, was to put together a training program that could help all my sales reps to understand at least the basics of server design.

I held two classes every Friday around lunchtime. Everyone brought in their own lunch and learned on their own time. In the first class, my newer reps received basic Enterprise training. The second class was for, but not limited to my more tenured reps, and that class was treated to relevant topics based on the issues and opportunities I had been seeing that week.

Although not a mandatory class, we typically had better than ninety percent attendance. Maybe that was because understanding servers and storage was essential to a rep's future at Dell. Maybe I was just that good a teacher. Or, potentially, it was the fact that my ISRs knew that those who still needed to figure out how to configure a RAID 5 to finish their quote would be the last ones I responded to before I left for the day.

I love to teach, so those sessions were great fun and highly energizing. They also allowed me to single-handedly support our fast growing Partner division through that first year. I remember when Stephanie, one of my reps, moved back to Direct. Her new manager stopped by my cube to marvel at, then thank me profusely for how thoroughly Enterprise-competent Stephanie was. More than a few of my ISRs went on to become TSRs themselves.

Soon enough, we split ISR support among a small team of TSRs, and I put together "The Enterprise Bible" for our combined classes. When I finally left Dell in 2017, I could still see a few of those binders sitting on the shelves at my old rep's desks.

One of the main things I remember from those early years of our new division, was how creatively and diligently our teams worked to show our VARs that partnering with Dell could be a winning formula for them.

Even on a simple desktop or laptop sale, it took time and effort to point out the fact that our rock-solid Optiplex desktops and Latitude notebooks boasted many advantages for businesses over our cheaper and flashier Dimension and Inspiron consumer lines.

It might be easier to just fill an order for a single Dimension desktop, but taking the trouble to ask a few probing questions helped our Partners sell products that really delighted their customers. In those early days, we were only getting a few percentage points of any reseller's business, so it typically had the added benefit of uncovering further opportunities.

Partners naturally came to us for desktops and laptops, so the focus was always on Enterprise. From training on how to uncover and recognize storage and other high-end opportunities, to bundling to gain new lines of business, every form of advertising and training you can imagine was used to encourage both our Partners and our own ISRs to focus on servers, storage, and eventually with the purchase of Force10, on networking.

It was considered the hardest job at Dell, and our Partner group was seen as a "black sheep" division by Direct for many years, but we still drew the best and brightest from Dell's ranks: Type A personalities who were not afraid of a challenge, salespeople wanting to prove themselves quickly for a management or field track, and those who were simply focused on breaking the (by then) quarterly bell curve as often as possible.

8. Building a Bigger, Better Ship

In 2008, Dell bought EqualLogic, our first large acquisition that was perhaps more Partner than Direct oriented. EqualLogic was a very successful, award-winning line of Storage Array Network, or SAN products.

SANs help customers consolidate storage. Instead of trying to manage the data on all the hard drives in many different servers, a SAN consolidates all those drives into a single place and allows users to manage them from "a single pane of glass," typically giving good to great performance gains along the way.

Up to that point, Dell had a very successful line of JBODs, which are dumb metal chassis with "Just a Bunch Of Drives" in them, and we partnered with EMC for our customer's higher-end storage needs.

EqualLogic was one of the most respected "smart storage" oriented startups. Michael Dell perhaps put it best when he told us, "We are not buying a hardware company, we're buying a brilliant software company."

I know I've always thought of EqualLogic as one of our best acquisitions. It brought in a whole new wave of Partners and helped our existing Partners understand how serious Dell was about doing business with them. Most importantly, EqualLogic was a jewel of a product. Compared to other SANs of the time, it was ridiculously easy to set up, super easy to scale, and always fast and dependable.

In the first days after this ground-breaking acquisition, the VARs who had been selling EqualLogic, but also HP and/or IBM, weren't calling Dell, so management put together a "business as usual" outbound campaign.

Our job was to call these potential Partners and let them know that, although they needed to register with Dell now, instead of through EqualLogic, Dell had already lowered the price of the entire product lineup for them. We also let them know Dell would be transitioning EqualLogic to Dell platforms going forward, with all the quality guarantees, associated global supply chain efficiencies, and build capabilities that implied. Finally, through the simple fact that the brand was now owned by a Tier One vendor, Equal-

Logic would enjoy greater advertising efforts and so broader recognition going forward.

Once we made the basic points, we then let them know that they had also been grandfathered in to our Partner program and could sell other Dell products. In the articles being published at that time by the main industry publication, *Computer Reseller News*, good price points and well-engineered products were the general themes of comments from resellers already selling Dell, so it was an inherently attractive offering.

Of course, we also mentioned Dell Direct tended to bring business to Partners who brought business to Dell, so the EqualLogic acquisition was really an opportunity for all our Partners, old as well as new, to do more, rather than less with Dell. Our bottom line proposition was, they should just consider this, "business as usual...with a few added benefits."

Truthfully, no one was quite sure how all the details of the processes were supposed to work in those first few weeks, but we made those outbounds with a will to win. We introduced ourselves, talked about what we could talk about, and took action items to find the answers for and get back to our new Partners ASAP on any concerns they were willing to verbalize. Just another day in the office for us. Just another growth opportunity for our still-youthful Partner division.

It wasn't merely our new Partners who were reacting cautiously to the EqualLogic acquisition. Many of the reps from the original EqualLogic sales teams, who were visiting all week that first week, were concerned they might lose their jobs, lose customers, or just lose out in general because of the acquisition.

I remember telling one rep, "Don't worry so much. Let's say you have ten EqualLogic dealers in your region. Get ready to double that number, because most of my existing Partners are going to start selling EqualLogic too."

I mentioned a call I had handled earlier that same day from a Dell Direct Rep. He had told me, "I've got a $350,000 EqualLogic deal I'm already working to close with your VAR. Let me ask you a question. Two to four months down the road, there's a two-and-a-half-million-dollar VMWare consolidation going on for that same customer, and we're fighting the fact that there's another VAR quoting the VMWare with HP. I'm wondering if your Partner might be interested in helping us lock that project up for Dell?"

Of course, that Direct rep was happy to bring the deal

to us, because the Partner helped strengthen Dell's position with that customer, and the rep still made the same commissions as if he had handled the entire project himself.

The Partner helped and made his dime off the deal, our "overlay" division handled the quoting, and everyone received credit. That was the genius of Michael Dell.

When he opened the Partner division, Michael decided he wasn't going to pay just one group, he was going to pay everybody. The TSR, the ISR, the AE, the SC, the manager—everyone in our Partner division who was involved got credit.

Our counterparts on the Direct teams also got credit.

Even the EqualLogic rep for that area got their piece of the action.

He could do that because none of us got paid commissions directly on revenues generated. It was counted as earnings against that old monster, Quota.

Whatever the Partner made was considered a cost of getting the business in the first place and, contrary to some reps' short-sighted opinions, our Partners added so much value that Dell not only won more often, we typically came out of Partner-led projects with more margin, rather than less.

That one decision underlay the entire evolution of our division's success over time. It's why we went from one team supporting every Partner in North America, to Partners owning and helping close a large percentage of the deals at Dell.

I always thought Michael opened the Partner division in the first place because the main weakness of Dell Direct was an ability to put feet on the street.

How could our own flyboys, supporting multiple accounts across large areas, compete on large projects and build more extended business relationships properly, when local resellers could, in effect, sit on a customer's doorstep every day and take the time to really get to know their business needs intimately?

We may have started out being "The Devil" as far as the Partner community was concerned, but because of that same single, simple decision, it was always a two-way street. Partners brought Dell business, and smart Dell reps brought Direct business to our Partners. After all, if they could get another division to do most of the work and a Partner to help close the overall deal, it freed them to focus on developing their other accounts.

Getting ahead by leveraging resources, it was and is just another good way for any Dell sales rep to break that old bell curve and make the big bucks.

9. Charting New Waters

It was the spring of 2010. As I crossed the vast parking lot supporting both Round Rock One and Round Rock Two, the sound of mowers and edgers filled the morning air. I worked in the central time zone, but an account set could be anywhere in the nation, and anyone who didn't have an early shift better be prepared for a walk. Since I supported West Coast accounts, I came in at nine o'clock every day, and it was a ten-minute stroll just to get to the lobby of our big building.

Dell was continuing a turnaround, with fourth-quarter financial results breaking records along the way. Everything was generally headed in the right direction, and everyone at Dell was pretty confident we were on the right track.

During this transformation period, my world had also changed quite a bit. I was pushing our new PowerEdge C Cloud products before most reps even knew they existed. That extraordinary set of products and the extraordinary team that supported them helped me earn some of my biggest paychecks in all my years at Dell.

Someone once claimed that if they cut me I'd bleed blue. The truth is, I just paid attention when opportunity knocked. Almost a year earlier, I'd been on a phone call with Glenn, one of our West Coast Storage Enterprise Technologists, when he said something pretty radical for a world that was, at that time, all about SAN storage. Glenn told me, "In the Cloud, it is not going to be about SANs, it's going to be all about DAS storage."

DAS, or Direct Attach Storage, really just means hard drives in JBODS or servers. As I reflected on his words over time, they made more and more sense to me. Why buy high-priced SANs when comparatively inexpensive servers with lots of cores, SSD drives, and high-speed interconnects could do all the front-end work, JBODs with larger, cheaper NLSAS drives could handle simple storage needs, and smart operating systems could provide the secret sauce that would load balance everything for highest availability?

The Silicon Valley companies I was supporting at that time, who were at the heart of the burgeoning world of Cloud services, were the first to adapt those DAS-oriented solutions en masse.

Cloud opportunities, hyper-scale computing, large purchases of hundreds or thousands of servers—seems when something like that pops up it would be obvious, doesn't it? But, in those early days, the Cloud could come at you from the strangest directions.

I remember an opportunity where I was on the phone with one of my Partner's sales reps and a customer. They wanted to buy about thirty R410s, an 11th generation economy server model that was current at the time. I addressed their requested memory configuration, like I always did when people detracted from their server's performance, by using non-optimal memory configs, and asked a simple question to help define the potential impact: "What are you using these servers for?"

The customer responded, "This is part of a pilot project. We're building out a Cloud like Amazon's." They said that once they finished their pilot phase, they were planning on buying thousands of servers.

I let them know, "If you are building out a Cloud, you may want to take a look at our PowerEdge C series Cloud servers." I went on to share some examples of the value of that particular line of products. Originally built for and available only to our largest Cloud customers, models like the C6100 boasted twenty-five percent more servers in the same space as a traditional blade chassis, at a much lower price point.

The cost savings alone made PowerEdge C the obvious choice for that customer, but they were equally enthralled with the features that had been custom built into the entire PowerEdge C line up, the very same features that had helped make those servers so attractive to the eBays of the world.

My Partner's sales rep didn't know what in the world I was talking about on that first call, and although he immediately called me back with questions and remained nervous about a product line that was new to him, it all worked out. That customer ended up being one of Dell's largest for several quarters, as they regularly bought PowerEdge C servers by the hundreds.

The Dell Custom Solutions group, or DCS, that helped with all projects involving the PowerEdge C series was, by itself, the third largest computer company in America that year.

DCS had connections throughout Dell and knew how to button down all the details of large projects. Their help was immensely valuable to our team. It also taught us much about the higher-end, more custom capabilities of the Dell machinery.

We learned to directly leverage those same capabilities for our Partner's benefit over the next few years and it made a huge difference in their focus on Dell. During the time we were on the account, we went from owning just a few percentage points of their business to helping generate more than half of that Partner's entire annual revenues.

In fact, we grew them into an LVAR, or Large VAR, one of the handful of top-rated Partners at Dell.

10. Diving with an "A" Team at LVAR Island

I want to stop and take a deep breath here. Although this is more of a memoir, a hopefully entertaining story of one person's experiences on the front lines of a high-tech company over a couple decades, it is not really about me. This is a story about Dell and the people that made Michael's company such an incredible place to work, over such a long period of time.

That was never truer than during the years I supported one of Dell's Partners with a true A-Team of highly talented people, a team whose competencies meshed almost perfectly, helping that Partner and their unique customer set grow business with Dell many-fold.

It was a few years into the building of the Partner division. Our growing group of TSRs was supporting about a dozen ISRs each. One of my ISRs was that rare slacker type who never lasts long at Dell. When he left the company, Tracy was assigned to his accounts.

Tracy had an abundance of charisma. Even when she

was in alligators up to her armpits, she always came out smelling like a rose. She was just that likable and that efficient.

Her entire Partner set started doing more business with Dell, but one Partner in particular, whose revenues had dwindled to just a few hundred thousand that year, increased their business dramatically over the years we were teamed together.

In fact, revenues grew to so many millions that eventually Tracy and I were assigned to handle just that one account.

A couple of years after we were dedicated to them, that same Partner hired Alvin as technical liaison for their field sales reps.

Alvin had been around the tech industry for a long time, knew just about everyone, and always seemed to be a step ahead of the rest of us. Alvin could take a large project from initial presentation, through the design and test phases, and to a successful conclusion faster and more efficiently than anyone else I've ever worked with. He had a natural genius that could do it all, and needless to say, he inspired great confidence in his customers.

He quickly became the go-to person for most of that Partner's existing and all of their new business.

That particular Partner specialized in hyper-scale customers. Because of the unique challenges those scale environments presented, we were advocating hard for an engineer who could become familiar with and help support Dell products in that more custom world of Cloud computing.

Dell came up with a creative way to support our request, the Partner committed dollars, and Fadi from Dell's Technical Support department joined, then quickly became the fourth member of our A-Team.

Fadi was a seasoned pro, with an almost intuitive grasp of the root cause of an issue. In the first few weeks, he resolved a couple of complex problems that had been dogging us for months, one of them threatening to cost our Partner a very large customer.

Then he created a campaign to effectively promote Open Manage Essentials for our Partner's largest customers. OME is one of those hidden free jewels at Dell that customers don't naturally gravitate to, but once they start using, end up loving. Because Dell designs and builds more highly engineered servers, system updates are more important than they are for simpler, more basic "white box" type servers. Coordinating needed updates is a real challenge for larger, more complicated infrastructures and OME greatly simplifies that process.

Implementing OME not only got rid of Dell quality perception issues in those huge server-oriented data centers, it also created a basis for belief in Fadi that let him go on to very efficiently handle new issues.

Their environments were so complicated, and those Silicon Valley companies needed to keep their processes so close to their vest, that previously when there was a problem, it more typically than not bogged down and could even take months to resolve. Because those customers had grown to trust him and more importantly, have faith in his ability to solve their problems, Fadi could often handle an escalating issue with a single call.

For Tracy and I, having Fadi on our team was like daylight at the end of a long dark tunnel.

The Partner's reps all loved Fadi too. I remember when a couple of their sales reps were tasked with building a new pipeline of customers in an untapped region of the country. They evangelized their dedicated support capability from Dell and the resolution miracles Fadi seemed to pull off regularly, and in just their first year, it helped them establish tens-of-millions in new revenue opportunities.

Tracy and I generated our own share of the success as well. We were pulling all sorts of levers at Dell to creatively meet our Partners' needs. It helped that the majority of their business involved multi-million-dollar projects.

In terms of bearing fruit, maybe the best single idea I had was to take some of the server seeds Dell was handing out, but the Partner didn't have a great use for, and move them into a Dell Solutions Center lab at the mothership.

That gave us access to Dell engineers and, since those Partner's server seeds were located on Dell premises, had the added bonus of implying a Dell rubber stamp for the many somewhat custom solutions we were engineering on the fly.

Basically, it came down to the fact that large projects always have problems. Solve whatever that customer was seeing as the key technical issues, and not only did that deal close more quickly, price bottlenecks were typically minimized. We soon earned the reputation of being problem solvers and business was brisk.

Over half that Partner's Dell revenues ended up running through our labs. When time was of the essence we could execute on a dime, so would supplement Dell resources and rustle up even more new customers from the Direct side of Dell.

Major vendors were also coming our way. They would send us components for specific projects and ask for help vetting that solution.

Fadi came into the lab after work all the time to help figure things out, and Alvin pitched in when he was in town. I took on the roles of procurer and project manager. By the end of our first year, we ended up being that particular Dell Solution Center's largest revenue generator.

Most of the time, our main competitors in projects were not HP or IBM, but wholesale houses like SuperMicro. We consistently beat them with our better-engineered products and services and made many happy customers along the way.

Those adaptive engineering efforts gave me a number of valuable insights and reminded me what has always been true: great products and services are more valuable to customers. Bottom line, you get what you pay for.

What I remember and love most about that part of my time at Dell, was the fact that I was part of an A-Team. I understand now why Steve Jobs made such a point of it. Put the right team together and you can change the world.

11. A Quick Tour of the Partner Side of the Ship

Try to imagine the breadth and depth of resources a company the size of Dell Technologies brings to the table: tens of thousands of smart, focused individuals, a global point of view, not limited to any one region, but pulling in best practices from all over the world—a company that is patent-rich and sits on many standards boards, a company that leads in so many areas it helps define the future. Partners should think of Dell as a giant ship of resources that can help their reach, exceed their grasp.

Dealing with Dell's many components can be as confusing as dealing with the government, but if you take the time and energy to learn what's available and how to leverage it (like some of Dell's sharpest Partners have done), you can build entire businesses around those resources. The amazing thing is, many of them are free!

Dell's subject matter experts are legion. They don't

cost you anything, you just have to know enough to reach out to them, and they are happy if you say, "Thank you!" (although it never hurts to acknowledge their contribution to their managers once the deal is done).

Of that group, the ETs or Enterprise Technologists are some of the best and brightest at Dell, and are a perfect example of the kind of resources you can leverage, with a little effort. They are highly experienced technologists who can go in-depth on a variety of subjects, solve complex design scenarios, guide you through potential minefields, and make complicated subjects clear and concise for customers. Think of them as super geeks with charisma.

I first engaged an ET many years ago for a Partner who was helping a bank climb out from under a heavy regulatory shadow. They needed expert guidance on Microsoft product legalities. I scheduled the call, our ET joined, helped resolve all that customer's Microsoft questions, then asked a few penetrating ones of his own.

He understood everything that bank needed to do to get compliant again and instilled such confidence with his grasp of the situation, that the bank ended up moving its entire project over to our Partner. Instead of handling a 300K piece of the action for Microsoft software, they ended up with the entire three-million-dollar project on their plate.

ETs have been helping enable my largest initiatives ever since. In my LVAR years, it was an ET who helped me germinate the idea for our labs, one of the most profitable enterprises we ever undertook for a Partner.

There's always been a ship full of experts at Dell, supporting everything from initial design to final implementation. Entire teams are focused on various technologies. There are even teams to keep straight and shepherd all the hundreds of details of large, complex orders through the manifold Dell processes, to ensure quick, clean delivery of that large project to a Partner or customer.

Experts aren't the only resources Dell can make available to you. I remember one initiative where we gave away almost a million dollars worth of equipment to introduce our new M1000 blades to our top Partners.

I had a small hand in that one, helping with the design of the blades and their chassis. Since blades were perfect for virtualization, I went to VMware and asked them for permanent copies of their software. I knew

I could get free server operating systems with Hyper-V from Microsoft, but VMware was the six-hundred-pound gorilla in the virtualization arena, so that was my preference.

VMware said, "We can do that," and gave us two and a half million dollars' worth of software for our blade seeds.

That was a great value-add to our Partners, helping them to build, play with, test, and demo real solutions for their customers. It was also, indirectly, an example of the power of Dell. I never had a problem getting other vendors to contribute product to meet any kind of real need. In fact, most of them were eager to do so.

That level of cooperation is not something Partners can accomplish easily on their own, but it is another very good way Dell, as a Tier One vendor, can "help a Partner's reach, exceed their grasp."

The truth is, it's hard to get a handle on the real extent of Dell's huge ship of resources. After twenty years, I was still learning how to leverage all the resources at my command, but Dell does have one other resource I just can't miss mentioning.

Executive Business Center (or EBC) conferences are

one of the best ways to nourish both customer and Partner objectives, help give direction to, and lock down large projects, or otherwise go in-depth on any specific subject a Partner (or customer) wants to know everything about.

Dell brings you into a state-of-the-art facility, dines you on a rich multi-course menu, and fills you with the rich technological capabilities it has to offer.

Dell has many EBC locations. Because I typically engaged a larger number of higher-end resources, I tended to use the one at the mothership in Round Rock, where most of those resources were already located. I put together over a dozen EBCs while I was at Dell. All of them were unique and tailored to meet particular needs.

One interesting EBC we did back in the early days of our Partner division was with (what was at that time) the largest IBM and VMware reseller in the nation. It was a tremendous company and very loyal to its vendors, but they had been having so many issues with IBM over such an extended period of time, that they were considering doing business with Dell instead.

It was a major shift for them, but one key reason they were willing to look at Dell was because of the way they worked. For any large project, they would scope that customer's needs, then present a single price tag for a complete, all-encompassing solution. If it was a million dollars total, that's the number they showed the customer. Since the hardware portion of the solution was part of the difference between the cost of and profit on any solution, no matter how big a dealer they were with IBM, Dell was going to get them the same quality hardware for less.

Also, Dell didn't have a big manual that said, "This is how a Partner has to do business with us."

Dell showed off our capabilities at that EBC, then our management negotiated, and ultimately established what turned out to be a great working relationship with a brand-new Dell Partner destined to do big business with us.

I remember another Partner whose customer was building three new data centers before the end of the year. They had several hundred servers and were headed toward several thousand.

Theirs was a valid way of doing things—a valid way to build out their operations—but in terms of costs, they were nowhere near as efficient as they could have been.

In their EBC, our experts dug into everything that customer was thinking.

Then, they left with our Partner's engineers in tow. They came back into one of the afternoon sessions with answers to every big question the customer had voiced that morning. They also came back in with solid recommendations for more efficient directions.

That customer had just come from two days in Houston with HP, but they signed with Dell and our Partner on the spot. Their main comment that sticks in my memory is, "HP only talked at us about how to most efficiently fill our orders."

I remember CTO-level information shares, architecture revamps, the groundwork laid for new solutions, and even (way back in the day) an entire team of engineers trained on how to migrate customers from Big Iron to the x86 platform.

If you have been to an EBC and been bored by PowerPoint slides, your Dell team may have missed the mark. Let them know what you really need and kick it up the ladder if needed.

No challenge is too big for an EBC to handle. On a couple of our largest projects, Michael even showed up to help. Just sayin'.

12. Wrapping up the Trip

Here are a couple of personal notes I kept that well embody the latter part of my journey, riding on the coattails of Michael's pioneering genius. They are from the days surrounding my twenty year anniversary...

Tracy helped kickstart the celebratory feeling Friday, at the beginning of my twentieth year at Dell, by sending four boxes of too sweet, cupcake-sized bundt cakes called "Bundtinis" to my desk. She added a stack of big, gaudy balloons that reached to the ceiling. One of my fellow TSRs told me later that she had IMed him asking if the balloons were obnoxiously large and showy. He said yes and she said, "Good, that's the effect I'm trying for."

Silly me, I didn't even think to be embarrassed. I just knew Tracy too well. Always a facilitator, she was announcing my anniversary to any and all, kick-starting the rounds of congrats and well wishes that would naturally follow. As I went about my day, generating quotes, supporting large customer concerns, and run-

ning projects out of the Dell labs, a sense of the occasion kept warming my heart. When I headed over to the Dell Solutions Center in RR3, I carried a box of the Bundtinis with me to share with our engineers.

I wouldn't have thought it possible, but that very next Friday outdid the small pleasures of my anniversary day with its exciting news. That morning, I was watching the opening session of FRS, our annual Field Readiness Seminar, an event that spans the Americas. Bill, president of the Americas, came to North America's Acquisition of the Year winners, and a PowerPoint detailing our own customer's data center buildout on Dell played across the stage's dual big screens. Since we were the core of the larger team responsible for that win, larger than life headshots of Tracy and I followed on those same screens.

I really enjoyed that fifteen seconds of fame (and the Platinum award that went with it), but the focus of the video accompanying that part of the presentation provided perhaps the most enjoyable moment for this long time Partner Division veteran, who had been there from the first. It highlighted the fact that our Partner first led us to, then helped carry the ball all the way through to that big win, and it finished with Bill telling everyone in that auditorium, "Either get a Partner to work with, or get left behind!"

I remember when Dell had been "The Devil" to the reseller community, no one on the Direct side wanted to work with Partners, and we were considered the black sheep division. We sure had come a long way in just a little more than a decade! That reward was a sweet reminder of the entire journey, but Bill's words spoke volumes about the future.

I had gone from selling a handful of servers to our entire Partner community that first month our new division was in business, to selling thousands of servers to a single Partner in a quarter, and even after twenty years aboard that mighty ship, I was still coming to work every day extremely excited about what I was seeing, and about what new miracles of progress were around the next corner.

One of my last paychecks at Dell, now Dell Technologies, was one of my best. I was supporting only one LVAR Partner, and our quota was many millions for that quarter, but in typical Partner division fashion, we blew out our number.

Most of the creative, really tough work, was done by the field team. My main job was to accurately pump out multiple quotes for hundreds of servers every day.

Michael and Betty, one of the finest field teams I've

worked with, were onsite at that Partner and in front of customers with them all the time, opening up new possibilities, putting out fires where needed, essentially building a trust factor that ultimately helped bring many of that Partner's largest global projects Dell's way.

Whether it was a massive POC that needed both product and engineering resources to help bring it to fast and successful fruition, custom support quoted for massive data centers of Dell equipment, global supply chain logistics that needed to be built out, or special financing that covered not just Dell, but all the products that Partner's customer needed for a project, the big Dell machine was mobilized and effectively employed by that veteran field team.

PART III
IN SUMMARY

Between my Direct and my Partner years, Dell was very, very good to me for over two decades, and it is still the best company I have worked for in my forty-plus years in the workforce.

I am a bit surprised there are not more books published about Dell. Beyond the many Silicon Valley companies that have made it big, the story of one Texas boy who started out at the age of nineteen with a thousand dollar investment, and because he just had bigger, better ideas and a terrific base of people to help execute them, is now one of the twenty richest men in the world, should be worth more print than what I've seen to date.

Although the facts are remarkable in their own right, I hope this memoir adds some further flavor from another Texan to what Michael himself has already written about his pioneering enterprise.

13. Michael

Back in 2008, I was at my desk one morning watching a meeting between Dell's execs and a roomful of analysts on my computer screen. Michael Dell was front and center, with Dell's top brass seated on either side of him. As they answered the analyst's questions, the execs kept preceding their comments with, "Michael said this," and, "Michael said that." My reflections from that morning include this interesting note…

"It's always good to have someone in charge, and Michael Dell is a person I've always felt really comfortable working for, both for his leadership capabilities and because he has a maverick genius for direction in this wide, wickedly competitive world of technology sales."

I remember everything that they were talking about that morning sounded momentous, but the truth is, large events and big changes have always been SOP (Standard Operating Procedure) at Dell, because Michael's company thrives on the cusp of change. In fact, an oft-repeated catchphrase of Dell's employees has always been, "Speed of Dell."

If it had been left up to IBM, an entire industry would've grown up around mass manufacturing processes that were convenient for the OEM, but not so much for customers. Michael Dell had a better idea. He figured out how to individually build every single Dell desktop and laptop to meet each customer's particular needs.

Then, he took his visionary strategy Direct, because he believed customers needed to be able to conveniently discuss, with a well-trained rep, what they wanted as well as what they really needed.

He built a direct marketing campaign through the mail with very streamlined, and easy to peruse catalogs of his products. The Dell name may not have been widely advertised, but everyone who bought Dell swore by Dell, so those little catalogs supplemented word of mouth to bring more customers Dell's way than the division I first worked for could (almost) keep up with.

The Internet came along, so he expanded those catalogs online and started pulling in business from everywhere.

As the Internet revolution kicked into high gear, everyone else was buying up technology startups in what looked more like a mauling than a merging, but Michael Dell's operations stayed lean and clean. Michael ignored the easy looking money, even refusing to finance products for the flakier Internet startups. When the revolution faltered, and so many companies failed, Dell sailed on.

Then Michael started building a bigger, better ship. He became acquisition-minded, and during that same period, the possibilities of our Partner division provided a fuel boost that is still speeding Dell into the future.

When he finally went private in 2013, Michael's company effectively became the largest tech startup in history. Here's a note I jotted in my journal from that time...

Bold moves? Yes.
Uncommon moves for a large corporation? Yes.
Unusual moves for Michael? No.

He fought that hard and complicated battle to go private for a multitude of very concrete reasons, but I believe there was one overarching purpose in his mind. Because he didn't have old product lines to protect, Michael wanted a laser focus on next-generation technologies. He needed to continue to invest for the future, not be beholden to the quarterly focuses of Wall Street. Even while technology shifts were accelerating dramatically, embedded public perceptions were hamstringing the need for change, so he changed the game.

Going private put his company years ahead of the competition.

Then, Michael did it again. In the largest tech acquisition in history, he bought EMC, almost doubling the size of Dell overnight!

This, from the same man who had resisted buying any other companies for the first two decades, only then carefully venturing into acquisition waters by systematically purchasing small to medium operations with a steady and strategic deliberation.

What justified that huge merger in his mind?

For one thing, Michael bought himself time. If the majority of Dell's SAN customers were small to medium businesses, companies that would naturally be the first to head for the Cloud, EMC's products were focused on medium to large corporations, including all the *Fortune* giants that would surely be the last to take that leap. And, since it's always all about the code, he also provided Dell with an extensive, high-quality code base to cover all contingencies.

What he really did, on the way to creating one of the largest technology providers on the planet, was to finally give Dell legitimacy as a real solutions behemoth. The types of FUD HP used to throw at us had become laughable. No one would ever again say, "Dell? Isn't that the little catalog computer company in Texas?"

Up to the point of that merger, there had been four great ages of computing: back at the beginning, mainframes ruled the world. Then came the x86 era, with its massive multiplying of computers. Everyone who could, did own a desktop, and corporate data centers sprawled across the landscape. Then, the third era, the age of virtualization freed compute from its physical limitations. The fourth age, "The Cloud," with its easy access and undeniable, irresistible economies of scale, was rapidly moving data away from conventional data centers.

With over a million employees, a monster called Foxconn was already helping design, then build and ship most products to the Dells, HPs, and Apples of the world. As economies of scale began forcing businesses more and more toward the services offered by giant infrastructure farms run by companies like Amazon and Microsoft, those same massive operations were starting to utilize Foxconn to design and buy their own custom versions of enterprise products.

It is no surprise that the EMC purchase bypassed those fast commoditizing, ultra-low margin portions of the market and focused on well-established brick and mortar giants.

If the umbrella of Dell Technologies gives Michael Dell enough advantages, I can easily imagine a future in which the owner of one of those mega data centers takes his, or her potential customer on a tour of their facility, and proudly points to the many rows of racked products with their blue-lit emblems boasting a crooked "E" as proof of the quality of innovation, the dependability, and the excellence of support they can offer that potential customer.

After all, the only real rule for technology is, "Everything changes," and the adage, "You get what you pay for" is as old as consumerism itself.

As I finish writing this chapter in mid-2018, the fifth age of computing is already almost upon us. Distributed computing, with its IOT (Internet of Things) foundation and AI (Artificial Intelligence) underpinnings are building a strongly prevailing headwind, which will inevitably, once again, help re-plot the course of many technology giants.

The good news for Dell? Michael is still at the helm, and his hand is firm on the wheel.

While I was writing this book, Kathleen, my editor, asked me an interesting question: "What is Michael's greatest strength?"

I immediately responded, "At how many other corporations do the employees call their CEO by his first name?"

Michael is still supremely involved with the company that bears his name. One day he might be on stage at a major conference talking in depth, with great clarity and precision, about any one of Dell's capabilities. The next, he might show up at someone's desk, take over the phone, and start selling a laptop to the next customer on the line.

In the twenty-two years I was there, everyone heard directly from Michael often and in detail, and he was always very open in his communications. That made it easy to match our goals to his, because we knew what he was thinking. I remember Michael summarizing one of his emails to us by writing, "We will be bold in our thinking and swift in our actions." That is Michael to a T.

Bottom line? Monster challenges versus Michael? I would and very profitably have bet my money on that crooked "E" every time.

14. Where I Did Not Go

Contrary to how this book may read, it was not a pleasure cruise. There were plenty of rough waters over the years, and working for a hundred and thirty thousand employee company is totally different than working for a five thousand employee company.

This book is not about the hard times. Nor, is it about the missteps, although over two decades there have been plenty of those. Moving our tech support to India, and building a service model that really worked—both problematic ventures—only became really advantageous to Dell over time.

Yes, sometimes it was a bumpy ride, but that's part of what made it so interesting.

What I really want readers to take away from this book is the amazing journey I was on for more than twenty years, courtesy of Michael Dell. Everyone who has worked for a living knows how extremely lucky I was to have had a job that was so fulfilling. So much more than just a job.

I've also skipped over some excellent personal memories that were part of, but not germane to the journey, like the Circle of Excellence trips I took for landing on top of the sales heap a few times over those two decades. The last one was to the Grand Caymans with my now-grown son. I made this note about that trip...

My son Kent and I are both sleepyheads. To bed before midnight, up by 8 am for me. Kent, at twenty, needs even an hour or two more to be fully fit to face the day. But, we were up by 7 am this morning to go get our passports. Kent forgot his driver's license, so we'll get up early and try again tomorrow. Milk run for our plane flight @ 6 am. We'll have to be up @ 3:30 or 4 am to make that one. Why even go to bed is my first thought? Piling up our sleep deposit, we have an 8 am shotgun start to play in a golf tournament our very first morning there.

The sad thing is, none of this scheduling is by our choice. The sadder thing is, this is supposed to be a relaxing reward for work well done. Think I will check into how much going a little earlier will cost. Getting there on our own terms has to be worth something, not to mention the value of having another few days in paradise.

We actually did go three days early, and with all the incredible experiences I had with my son, and my Dell family, that decision helped make it a most memorable trip indeed.

More than anything else, I have to confess I worked with so many fun and inspiring folk over the years, I could turn this neat little memoir about an incredible journey at an amazing company into a big fat book of stories. If this one is well received, maybe the next book I write will tell some of those tales.

15. Disembarking the Dell Ship

After twenty-two years on that highly profitable and almost always enjoyable voyage, I left the Dell ship to take on a slightly different challenge, one that was still well within my wheelhouse. My new job was to help one of Dell's largest Partners figure out how to do more business with Dell, and it ended up entailing quite a shift in perspective.

I've always said that Dell's Partners live in a larger world, but I didn't really comprehend what that meant until I was there, immersed in their business and their culture. It was like learning to think in Spanish.

In Texas, I hear Spanish spoken all the time and can generally make myself understood, but I am an inarticulate greenhorn compared to someone who can think in that language. To become that proficient I would have to go and live in Spain or Mexico for a while.

That's essentially what I did in 2017 when I joined that Partner's team.

Dell had been my whole world. For a Partner, Dell is just one component of the big, wide world of technology they have to master.

And nothing works the same way it does at Dell. When the world doesn't know your name marketing, lead generation, all revenue producing activities have to be approached in a more hands-on way and still, dollar for dollar, often produce far fewer results.

As for my fellow employees, some of the most important things I had to come to know and understand to be helpful (versus distracting) in my new role promoting Dell "at" instead of "to" a Partner, included:

The sales reps had vendors coming at them from every direction. They had to thoroughly understand and be able to message everyone's Kool-Aid, as well as be very articulate about their own company's value proposition.

The sales engineers had to deal with, and design for the daunting complexities of heterogeneous environments. It's one thing to deal with a single manufacturer's products, quite another to get different brands of equipment with divergent and proprietary coding working seamlessly together.

Everyone had to know their own customers intimately. Sales reps had to stay right on top of the pulse of a project, or their sales engineers would never get a chance to shine. Making new true believers out of, and building sound relationships with that next potential long-term customer required an almost uncanny sense of what was really needed and a coordinated finesse of execution that those teams managed to pull off every day, with almost pinpoint accuracy and audacious speed.

As for the Executives?

I never hesitated to reach out to any exec at Dell who could help one of my Partner's with a large project, but the VPs and Directors at my new company were so busy, I learned to think twice about even copying them on emails. My best guess is they were all getting hundreds of them every day. At Dell, it was considered polite to send an email before reaching out. At this new job, my better bet was always just to pick up the phone and call.

I thought I was busy at Dell; in my new position, it never stopped. There was no big team of people to help, so I could and often did work well into the evening, seven days a week, on everything that needed to be done. Often, I found myself having to use my own initiative to make the command decisions that would keep a project moving forward. Even so, I never could quite catch up.

It's not like the big Dell ocean liner, where every process is templated, everyone has their own swim lane, and the ship only turns in big arcs. It was more like being on a racing schooner. Everyone was nimble and everyone was quick because every day was an obstacle race.

Differences aside, my company employed the same type of high-quality individuals I loved working with at Dell, and they showed the same kind of absolute loyalty to their company. In a very different way, it was just as exciting as Dell, and once I had retrained my thinking, I began to figure out how to make a difference.

For my role, as a bridge builder with Dell, it still came down to the same basic truth I had been evangelizing for years: "Dell is a giant ship of resources that can help your reach, exceed your grasp."

Helping enable everything Dell was just half the value of my job though.

The other half was helping both my own and Dell's sales teams, navigate the projects they were working on together. That part of my job was an immediate, bottom line difference maker, and it was a very comfortable, fun thing for me to do—something I was well prepared for after many years helping build Dell's Partner division from the ground floor up.

If I was making a list of the most important things I accomplished while there, I would start with all the Dell and EMC gear I obtained for their labs, but second on that list would be helping expand their relationship with Dell's OEM group.

Yes, there is an OEM division within the larger OEM that is Dell. They are responsible for the more custom solutions that Partners and customers require to either bring a product to market or bring a specific project to fruition.

Since this Partner was also often focused on larger customers with custom needs (the same way our lab at the Dell Solutions Center did), the OEM group helped provide the value-adds needed to win our largest projects.

The bonus was there were only about three hundred folk in that entire division, so it made for a neater, cleaner overall partnership than the much larger Direct side of Dell could offer.

One of the other interesting ways I ended up helping

was through the videos I made (by leveraging Dell resources, natch). During our national sales convention, one rep took the time to take me aside and tell me that the very first video I produced had helped introduce him properly to both the customer and the Dell Direct team, and get him quickly into the strategic middle of a massive new project.

The truth, as I have come to understand it, is that videos have an inordinate amount of power to make a smaller company's capabilities real for potential customers. If many other forms of marketing proved not to be as effective as they would have been for a name brand like Dell, videos were, and perhaps are, more central to and essential for Partners, than even for Dell. After all, at Dell we got by with a factory full of candy-colored laptops and "Dude, you're getting a Dell" for years!

There has to be some kind of lesson about being a bottom line, no question about it, revenue-generating sales rep, versus having any other role in a company, but after twenty-two years on the front lines at Dell, even as my next project (a series of data-driven initiatives) was getting off the ground, a company reorganization eliminated my more behind-the-scenes support position, just shy of my one year anniversary.

Even in that short time I directly, or indirectly, made enough of a difference to leave with the knowledge that I had made real contributions and been worth the money they paid me. The bonus was, I learned a new language, "Partner Speak," which gained me a more balanced perspective and a more unique value to the marketplace.

Afterword

I am an idea-oriented personality. I see a problem and my mind goes to work to solve it.

For example, one time I received feedback from a Partner's sales engineer. He said he would never focus on Dell switches, because there was no associated training track, like CISCO had for their switches, that would help him career-wise.

Dell's internal training programs were pretty basic at the time: one-off certifications, not any sort of career-conducive curriculum. That engineer started me thinking about what a higher seat of learning would look like at Dell, and the relevance it could have for both Dell employees and the industry in general. The required components fit together neatly in my head, and although Dell has come a long way with their training programs in the many years since, my notes on "Dell U" made sense for the time…

- *Dell University will be a more dynamic, organic environment*
- *Progress will be based on and structured around needs for knowledge*

- Managers will be responsible, as well as rewarded for nurturing their people's progress through this educational system
- Certifications will have meaning to the larger tech world
- Certifications will become an investment in an AE/SE/Tech's future, just as Cisco certifications are today
- Dell University will naturally extend into research and development, in addition to the understanding and repair of Dell products
- The future of Dell will begin to evolve through Dell University
- Coherence will be found in a centralized, virtual campus
- Master ETs will be in charge of content for each area

Many ideas have come and gone over the years, some implemented, others just grist for the mill. Way back when Cloud was still an early adopter market, Dell wasn't getting a lot of traction with our own prepackaged solutions. One of the execs asked me how our LVAR Partners could potentially help. I responded with these thoughts:

Why lock ourselves into a few offerings and push

against a marketplace that is not ready for Prime Time? Why not focus on leveraging a number of solutions through our Partners, using the experience and capabilities they've already built around their own specializations...

- Let our Partners incubate specific solutions and reward them with a piece of the action

    ◦ Minimizes our own investment, but we still leverage our engineering and supply chain expertise to help button down the solution
    ◦ We can help wrap security, integration (particularly with their IT), and leverage Public Cloud as a safety valve to excite customers who are leery of Cloud (most of our target audience)

- Create the Cloud-oriented Reference Architecture templates needed for each solution and commoditize them for our customers
- Dell Financial Services packages can help make these minimal risk purchases
- We keep adding to our one big house and trying to get people to come, but Cloud products are evolving rapidly

- Ex: Every time we think we can lock down OpenStack, it has already evolved again
- Better to build smaller houses in PG and meet needs of the market before the market moves on
- OpenStack, not as an exception, but as an example of the rapidly evolving market means supporting solutions Directly is a slippery slope

I guess I will always be a problem solver, even a maverick at heart. Maybe Michael could create a brain trust with a bunch of us who approach problems from more intuitive directions, then call on us to wrestle with his more unsolvable-looking issues. The frontier days of Dell may be long gone and the company a large, diverse, and very civilized globalscape, but mavericks can still play a part.

For that matter, when asked by a reporter after he took Dell private, how long it would take to get a particularly good idea processed through the machinery and enacted at his company, Michael's response was emblematic of his own personality. He said, "Let me check with the board on that," then he gazed off into the distance for a moment, turned back to the reporter, and responded with a smile, "OK, that's done." Michael himself is still large and in charge and, I believe, still very much a maverick at heart.

THE END

Author Note

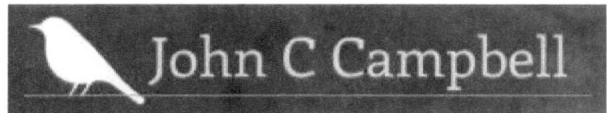

We hope you've enjoyed this Kindle production of *Riding on the Coattails of Genius*. If you are so inclined, please leave a quick review on Amazon. Reviews help!

The Audible production of *Riding on the Coattails of Genius* is narrated by the author and is available at audible.com.

Now that the book I've been wanting to write for twenty years is complete, I am doing consulting work with other Dell Partners facing the same challenges I've been helping solve for more than a decade.

Writing and video production opportunities are also taking up more and more of my day.

Thecreativenow.com is a central gathering place for all author and reader activities. Cool stuff is going on there all the time. "Sign-Up" to gain access to exclusive news and updates, enjoy bonus content, and see what's coming up next.

Final Note:

I love feedback. You are my readers and how this book helped or entertained you means everything to me. Have questions or strong feelings? Join us on the "FORUM" at thecreativenow.com and you are welcome to toss in your two cents. There is one forum just for fans of this book. I will be there too.

~ John C. Campbell

www.ingramcontent.com/pod-product-compliance
Lightning Source LLC
Chambersburg PA
CBHW021449210526
45463CB00002B/704